Flash, Bam, Alakazam

A play

Sue Wilding

Samuel French — London
www.samuelfrench-london.co.uk

FOR AMATEUR PRODUCTION ENQUIRIES

UNITED KINGDOM AND WORLD
EXCLUDING NORTH AMERICA
plays@samuelfrench.co.uk
020 7255 4302/01

Each title is subject to availability from Samuel French,
depending upon country of performance.

FLASH, BAM, ALAKAZAM

First presented by the Sedgefield Players at the Sedgefield Drama Festival on 24th September 2010 with the following cast:

Elsie   Norma Neal

Directed by Walter Howell

CHARACTERS

Elsie

The action takes place in Elsie's living room

Time—the present

For Jamie 1975 — 2005

FLASH, BAM, ALAKAZAM

Music plays: "Puff the Magic Dragon" by Peter, Paul and Mary

As the play opens, Elsie is sitting in a chair reading a newspaper

Elsie That model's on the front page again. Her that was in the jungle. It's all you've got to do these days, to get yourself famous. Sit in a house for ten weeks, eat giraffes' testicles or have sex with a footballer. Stars aren't proper stars, these days. You would never have seen Ava Gardner or Rita Hayworth getting out of a taxi with their drawers on show.

She looks out of the window

The removal van's loaded up now. Some of the neighbours are coming out to wave them off. I shan't bother. People make such a fanfare out of everything these days. Nobody just gets on with things. They're moving to Kent, apparently. Kent. They've got a long drive. I've got a tin of shortbread biscuits for them in the kitchen. Orange and almond, I made them myself. I thought they could eat them in the car. I'll give them to her when she pops across to say goodbye.

She looks down at the paper again

Someone thinks they might have spotted that little girl, the one that went missing. It'll be another false alarm. Jessica went missing once. In Woolworth's. She was there one minute, holding my hand. I let go, to get my purse out, and when I felt for her hand again it wasn't there. I do actually think ... I do actually think my heart stopped, just for a second or two. It actually stopped, I swear. Then I saw her, over by the pick and mix. And it started again.

She looks out of the window and is startled. She stands up

Oh! It's gone! The removal van's gone, so's their car.

After a moment, she sits down again

Oh well. All the more shortbread for me, then.

A noise, off. Elsie glances out of the window

Postman.

Lights fade

Elsie exits

Lights up

Elsie enters with a tray containing a small teapot, china cup and saucer, milk jug, a plate of biscuits and a letter in an airmail envelope. She sits down

I used to go to the coffee morning down at the church every Wednesday. I don't go any more. Well, it's a waste of money really. Why do I want to traipse all the way down there and pay one pound twenty for a cup of weak coffee and a Rich Tea, when I can sit in the comfort of my own home and have decent tea and home-made biscuits? The women are friendly enough, I suppose, but they do yack on and on about such boring things. Jessica says I should be getting out more. She says, "Mother, if you don't keep your social contacts, you're more likely to end up with dementia." Ridiculous. Sudoku and the quick crossword, they keep my brain sharp. And I like to read.

She pours herself some tea

Jessica writes to me every fortnight. She wants me to get on one of these computer things where you ... what does she call it? ... Chat on line. I don't want to chat on line. I like to hear a letter plop onto the mat, feel its heaviness in my hand. I've always liked to read. When I was little, I was the best in the class, but back then you weren't supposed to blow your own trumpet. Children now, they get praised for everything they do. In those days, you were never praised. It was always, "Well, Elsie, you read well, but so does little so-and-so and that fat girl with the birthmark." The only praise I got was from the headmistress, Mrs Ward. She used to call me to her office every Friday morning and I'd read from Little Black Sambo or Prince Caspian. And she'd give me a lollipop and say she'd never heard a child read so well. I felt special. Just for those few minutes.

She sits back, the letter on her knee, and has a sip of tea

The first time that happened, when I came home and told my dad how well I'd read, he told me not to be such a conceited little mare, and sent me out to clean my bike which he said was filthy. My mum said, "He's right, Elsie, it doesn't do to get above yourself." Shame things aren't like that now. I got no praise, no compliments. Never did me any harm.

She looks out of the window

There's that young girl from down the road. Anna. Comes past here every day with the pushchair. She called in once, when her little boy kicked his football into my garden. Had a cup of tea with me. We said we'd make it a regular thing, but ... well. I suppose she doesn't have time, with a five-year-old and a baby. I've seen her going into Tanya Morton's house most days. It looks like she's ignoring the warnings I gave her about that Tanya Morton. She had intimate relations with her husband's cousin. I told Anna, I gave her the low-down on everybody down this street. Tanya with her little affair. Betty Forbes with the son. You know. (*She looks around, as if someone can hear her*) He's a not-right. It's all very sad, but he's a bit frightening when he suddenly shouts like he does. Scares you to death. Husband left her, couldn't cope. Then there's that couple at number four. Barry and Chris. I wouldn't swear to it, but I think they might be ... you know ... that way. They have a lot of parties. Anna said she didn't really like gossip. Her little boy's got a lazy eye.

She has a bite of a biscuit and a sip of tea

And now I'm getting some new neighbours over the road. I shall keep my distance.

With a contented sigh, she carefully opens the letter

Jessica moved to Australia ten years ago. She married a doctor. A surgeon, should I say. Very high up, he is. They've got three beautiful children. Well. I say beautiful. I presume they are. I've never seen two of them, except in photos. And little Saskia, she was only two when they emigrated.

She reads from the letter

"Dear Mum. Well, it's non-stop here as usual, so this will be a bit brief, I'm afraid. Saskia wanted to thank you for the cheque you sent for her birthday, but she never seems to have time. I'm always saying to Ed, her social life is better than ours!" See. "Social lives", children have now. Saskia cried when we saw them off at the airport. She was all excited one minute, seeing the aeroplanes and all the people, and Ken had bought her a new teddy bear to take on the plane with her. She kept going up to people and showing it to them — "Gand-and bought me this." Gand-and. She couldn't say Grandad, then. She sat on Ken's knee ... and then the flight was called. The last I saw of Saskia, she was looking back at me over Ed's shoulder and asking why Gand-and and Gamma weren't coming. Then it suddenly dawned on her and she started to cry. She was distraught. Held her little arms out to us, but they'd gone through the gate by then. And it was too late to hug her.

Pause. Elsie is upset at the memory

That's what breaks my heart really.

Pause

She cried her little eyes out. Jessica told us she cried for Gamma and Gand-and through most of the flight. And now … well, now what do we have? Stilted conversations on the phone at Christmas, and on my birthday. And she can't even remember Ken.

Pause

That's what breaks my heart.

She recovers and becomes brisk

Still. Still. It's the way of the world. We move on.

The Lights fade to black-out

Music plays: "Who's Afraid of the Big Bad Wolf" by Henry Hall

The Lights come up. Time has moved on. Elsie is wearing a different cardigan or apron, something to signify that it's a different day. She has a very slight air of excitement about her, as she stands looking out of the window

The new people are moving in. It's there now, the removal van. I haven't seen them yet. Their car's there — one of those big jeep-style things. And I've seen a dog, a little Westie. If he comes onto my garden there'll be trouble. Those big jeeps ... they usually mean children, don't they? I've made some shortbread. It's proving to be quite a week. What with the new neighbours, and the big fanfare down the street last night. They had a party for young Ben Samuels, number eighteen's boy. He's been on one of those programmes, you know. One of those things where Andrew Lloyd Whatsit's looking for a star. He's after finding an Artful Dodger. Ben went to audition, he's through to the semi-finals. So they had a do at the village hall. I thought I'd better show my face. I mean, the neighbours have been putting up posters for weeks. "VOTE FOR BEN". His mother came round and asked me to put one up. I took it from her, but I threw it out. They play havoc with your windows. Ken put one up, years ago when they were building the bypass. We all protested against it. "BOO TO THE BYPASS", it said. I was scraping bits of paper off the windows for about three years after we took that poster down. So I didn't put up "VOTE FOR BEN". I doubt if his mother noticed. All this hoo-ha. Ridiculous.

She looks out of the window

The dog's there again. He's by the removal van, weeing on the tyres. Anyway, those things do no good. Posters. They went ahead and we got the bypass.
Pause

I went down to the do. For Ben Samuels. He's a bit of a show-off. They'd rigged up a little stage for him, and some music, and he sang "Consider Yourself Our Mate". Everybody clapped as if Jack Wild himself were up there singing. Such a shame about Jack Wild. Losing his life like that, so young. I had a word with young Ben afterwards. He was coming round collecting praise from everybody. Everybody was telling him he was going to win. I said, "You sang very well, but don't get your hopes up — there'll be others that are as good as you, and some that are better." That's what my parents would have said to me when I was his age. Well — you have to expect disappointment in this world, he needs to learn that. Ken used to say, "Hope for the best and expect the worst". I agree with him. But without the "hope" bit.

A doorbell rings, off. Elsie is visibly startled, then looks highly suspicious

Nobody ever rings my bell.

Elsie exits as the Lights fade

The Lights come up again

Elsie enters, looking bemused but quite pleased, holding a small card. She sits down and examines it

I've just met the new neighbours' little boy. That was him at the door. I'm surprised he could reach the bell ... he's a tiny little thing really. He gave me this card. It says, "My name is Jamie. My mummy and daddy are moving into number fifteen today. They would very much like to meet you. Please come for tea at three o'clock tomorrow." Isn't that nice? He's not written it, of course ... but still ... it's a novel way of meeting your neighbour.

She looks out of the window, and does a double-take

Oh. He's knocking on doors over the road now.

She is disappointed, but recovers quickly and tells herself off

Well, of course he is. They're not just going to invite me, are they?

She examines the card, suspiciously

I wonder what they're after? People don't do things like this normally, in my opinion. There was Jean McGee once, I met her down at the surgery. We got chatting. She came round a few times, but I didn't encourage it. She just wanted to have a nose round my house, that's all it was. I told Jessica about it on the phone. She laughed and said, "Mother, did it occur to you that she might just like you?" I said no, it hadn't occurred to me. Jean invited me round to hers, but I didn't like to be a bother. People don't mean it, really, they're just being polite. I haven't seen her for ages.

Pause

I wonder if they've got any other children. I hope not. I can't deal with children these days. Modern children. So noisy, so full of self-belief ... No. I won't go. They've got enough on, moving in, without the neighbours adding to it.

Pause

He's a sweet little boy though ... Jamie. Nice name.

Black-out. Music plays: "Nellie the Elephant" by Mandy Miller

Elsie exits

Two mornings later. The Lights come up again

Elsie enters, wearing a dressing gown. She has a tray of tea and toast. She settles herself down

Well, I think I've proved my point.

She pours herself some tea

I made a total fool of myself yesterday. I should have listened to myself, gone with my instincts. But no. Against my own better judgement, I went over there, to the new neighbours'. I made a big lemon drizzle cake, and took that with me. I was surprised by how many people were there. Mrs Armitage took a carrot cake, but it was shop bought, I could tell. I think mine was the only home-made cake there.

Pause

I felt them all looking at me when I walked in. They don't see much of me, that's why. I could tell they were all wondering why I was there. Anyway. The hosts were charming. Adrian and Kate, they're called. And of course there's young Jamie, he was there. Kate was saying they've got big plans for the house, they're going to have a conservatory. I said they should get the pond filled in, the one in the back yard. I think it could be dangerous for kiddies. She said they might think about it later, they've got so much to do.

She eats some toast and drinks some tea

I think I had a bit too much of the Buck's Fizz that Adrian was handing out. I thought it was just orange juice.

Pause

Do you like cats? I'm not so keen. I don't trust them. But they sense it, don't they, when you don't like them, and they come and sit on your knee. And that happened yesterday. Only it was little Jamie. Everyone was making a fuss of him. Not me — I don't think it does children good to get too much attention. Anyway, he was going round asking people to sing to him. One or two of the women sang him a nursery rhyme. Mrs Baker tried some songs from Mary Poppins. Ridiculous. She'd been on the wine, she couldn't control her teeth! When she sang *Supercalifragilisticexpialidocious* she spat all over the poor child! I was embarrassed for her.

Pause

Eventually he came to me. He asked me if I could sing. I said no, I wasn't very good. He looked disappointed, but life's about disappointment, he'll learn that. And I would have left it there, if I hadn't distinctly heard Mrs Armitage say, "She wouldn't crack her face long enough to sing that child a song." And I felt something snap inside me. And I sang Jamie a little thing that my mother used to sing to me. It's daft really.

After a moment she shyly sings the first verse of "Orange-Colored Sky"

She flaps her hand, dismissively

Anyway. A few people laughed. Jamie looked startled. I went home after that. It was the Buck's Fizz. Mind you, I had a really good night's sleep. But now I'm wondering what they must all have thought of me. (*She is upset*) You see, this is what happens when you venture out of your own space. It isn't good. When Ken was alive, we always had our meals in the kitchen. I wonder what he'd say if he saw me now, having breakfast in here. There's no point, though, is there? ... no point in setting the table just for me.

The doorbell rings. Elsie is startled

Who's that at this time?

She starts to get up, then thinks better of it

It's better when you keep yourself to yourself. I've proved it.

The doorbell rings again a few times but Elsie calmly eats her toast

The Lights fade to black-out. Music plays: "Little Boy Fishing" by Shirley Abicair

Elsie exits in the black-out

Still in the black-out, Elsie enters, this time without the dressing gown

A few days later. The Lights come up on a bit of a mess. A bright tin, open on the floor, buttons spilling out of it. An untidy pile of old comics. Elsie's china cup, and a mug with "World's Best Grandad" printed on it. A biscuit barrel. An enormous bunch of keys

Elsie is tidying up, but looking very cheerful and sprightly.

My little visitor's been round again. He does leave a mess. That was him, the other day, ringing the doorbell. Jamie. He was with his mum, Kate. I answered it in the end, they wouldn't go away. Do you know, when I first answered the door, my heart started to pound, because she said it was that song I sang to him. I just knew I'd offended them in some way. Anyway ...

She sits down

... it turned out, Jamie had been asking questions about the song and driving Kate up the wall. He wanted to know what it was that came out of the sky — why did it go flash bam alakazam? And why was the sky orange-coloured? Bless him. He was fascinated. Well, I had no choice, I had to invite them in. And now he keeps coming back. Every morning, without fail, he turns up on my doorstep. I'm a bit worried, actually. Yesterday, I saw him coming across, and I heard Kate shout after him "Don't you go pestering Mrs Hunter for too long, Jamie." She probably doesn't want him to come over.

She picks up the tin and starts to put buttons back in it

I've had this button tin all my married life. I never really take much notice of it. But Jamie found it and took it down, and I made the mistake of saying to him, "Every one of these buttons has a story to tell." Well, that did it. He wants to know the story behind every one. It'll take us forever. The button from my first pair of Biba flares. And this one — this one came off Dickie Valentine's shirt when a few of us mobbed him at the Gaumont in nineteen fifty-six. (*She picks up a button and smiles*) Ah. This one I can't tell Jamie about. It flew off my dress on our honeymoon, when Ken got a bit previous in the hotel lift. You can't tell a child that. I'll make something up, when he comes to that one.

She picks up the mug

He always asks for real cocoa. He's fascinated by it. Kiddies today, they're used to everything being instant, in sachets. He took the cocoa box down off the shelf and said "What's this, Esslie?" He calls me Esslie, bless him. I said it was cocoa and he had a sniff of it and said it smelt yummy. So I had to make him some. And now, every time he comes round, he has to have cocoa. Proper, rich, good-tasting cocoa that makes you warm inside. I whisk it, because he likes froth. And he always wants it in Ken's mug. Saskia gave Ken this mug, just before they emigrated. And these ... (*She starts to collect the comics together*) ... these were Ken's as well. Some of them date right back to the fifties. He was like a big daft kid. I used to say ...

She is suddenly overwhelmed with sadness

... I used to say, "You're like a big daft kid, with those comics." Dennis the Menace and him that used to eat cow pies, and the Bash Street Kids and Billy Bunter. They'll be worth a bob or two now, but I'll never sell them. And now they're getting a new lease of life, because Jamie loves them. Ken would be so pleased. I didn't keep much, when he died. And the stuff I did keep, people wouldn't understand. Like the comics and the mug. Things that meant something in here. (*She indicates her heart*) Things that only I knew. The jam jar he used to keep panel pins in. Nineteen sixty-three, I bought that jar of jam. And hanging in the hall, his hat. His trilby hat, that he always wore, rain or shine ...

She picks up the bunch of keys

These keys. Ken kept them in a drawer in the kitchen. Wouldn't let me chuck them out. He had no idea what doors they opened, what cupboards. He just liked having them there. He used to say, "You never know." Jamie likes to hang them on his belt loop and pretend he's a policeman. It's having nobody to talk to that leaves the ache. Nobody to talk to about what's happening in the world, and what's happening in my life. Jessica says, "You don't do enough, Mum. You should get out there." But what's the point in doing things, when I've got nobody to tell all about it when I get home? Sitting up in bed at night, putting my hand cream on, telling Ken about my day. Marriage comes in sachets too, these days. Just add water. Give it a stir. And if it goes cold, pour it down the sink. My Ken ... my Ken was a cocoa husband. Anyway. Listen to me. I'd better get on!

The Lights fade to black-out. Elsie continues to tidy up. Music: "Bring Me Sunshine" by Morecambe and Wise

Elsie exits in the black-out

The Lights come up

Elsie comes back in, wearing a coat with a handbag over her shoulder, holding a sandwich that she has bought, and a carrier bag. She flops into the chair. She looks harassed and very cheerful

I know. Look at me, with a bought sandwich. I used to think that was the height of laziness. I used to say to Ken, "Why do people buy ready-made sandwiches? Are they too idle to make their own?" But I'm so busy these days!

She unwraps the sandwich and checks herself for a second

Plate. Oh, sugar it, I can't be bothered.

She takes a bite of the sandwich and pauses for a moment

That's better, I'm getting my breath back. Wooh! It's been non-stop. When Kate came to pick up Jamie last week, she invited me for tea. I would have said no, I don't like to be a nuisance. But Jamie was desperate for me to go, he wanted to show Esslie his bedroom. So I went. And while I was there, they asked me if I'd mind babysitting. I felt a bit let down. It dawned on me then — I thought, ah, this is why she asked me over for tea. But never mind, it meant I could spend an evening somewhere different. They were going into town, to see a show, then for a meal. It was their fifth anniversary. I said, "Don't you worry about being late back, you take your time, I've nothing to rush home for." I had a lovely evening. Kate said, "We've left you some fruit and cheese, Elsie." Well! I was amazed. I imagined a bit of cheddar and an apple, but there was all kinds. Swiss cheese, runny cheese, blue cheese ... slices of melon and some strawberries and mango. I took my book, but I don't think I even picked it up. They'd only been gone five minutes when Jamie appeared, doing the "I want a drink of water" trick that children have used since time began. I wasn't fooled. But it was lovely to have him there, cuddled up to me, all warm in his pyjamas. I sang him some songs he'd never heard. *Gilly Gilly Ossenfeffer Katzenellen Bogen by the Sea.* He loved that one. And the one about the lonely pup in a Christmas shop. I shouldn't have done that, actually, it made him cry. But I cheered him up with *High Hopes.* (*She recites the last two lines of the first verse of "High Hopes" by Frank Sinatra*) Such richness. Little Jamie. That child has brought such richness into my life.

She recovers, and briskly opens the bag, pulling out a brightly coloured lunch box which she holds up

He starts school next week. So I've got him this. Kate said it was the one he wanted, so I said, "Well, let me buy it for him." He's not a spoilt child, you see. When they're not spoilt, you want to give them things. I'm taking it over there in a minute. Kate's going to hide it from him till just before he sets off to school on Monday. She's invited me over, you know — she's going to surprise him with the lunch box, and let me walk to school with them on his first day. I can't wait.

Something dawns on her. She looks sad

But I'll lose him then, won't I? Once he gets to school and finds lots of other kiddies to play with. Jessica went from clinging to me every morning, to saying, "Don't hold my hand now, Mummy" when her friends appeared. It'll happen to Jamie. He won't care about Esslie and the button tin and the silly old ram who thought he'd punch a hole in a dam.

She brushes the crumbs off her lap and looks in her bag for a tissue to wipe her hands

Puff the Magic Dragon. Another one of Jamie's favourites.

She sings the first three lines of the penultimate verse of "Puff the Magic Dragon" sadly as she wipes her hands. Her voice tails off, but then she recovers

I can't remember the rest. It's a daft song anyway. But Jamie likes it. I'll have to try and remember the ending for him. Anyway. I haven't time to sit here feeling sorry for myself. I've things to do. I'm taking this lunch box over to Kate, and then we're going down to feed the ducks.

She stands, starts to exit, and checks herself

Bread. I knew there was something.

Black-out

Elsie exits

Music: "Gilly Gilly Ossenfeffer Katzenellen Bogen by the Sea" by Max Bygraves

Monday morning

The Lights come up on Elsie standing looking out of the window, in her dressing gown. She looks sad, defeated

I don't like September. Even when it's sunny, like today, there's always a little chill, a warning of worse to come.

She turns, and we see that she has been crying as she sits down

I told them about that pond. I warned them, the day they moved in. I knew Jamie would be drawn to it eventually, he's such a curious little soul. Oh, if I could turn the clock back. But this is what happens, when you let people in. My instincts were right. I should never have allowed myself to get friendly with them. Grief's the price we pay for love, they say. But it's a bloody high price. Sorry. Language. They invited me round for home-made lemonade in the garden, it was a lovely afternoon. Adrian was up a ladder, doing something to their guttering. Kate and I sat in deckchairs watching Jamie playing, and the little dog running around. The lemonade was a bit tart for me; the sort that makes you close one eye. But it was nice just to be there amongst it all, feeling like part of the family. Then the phone rang and Kate went into the house. Jamie shouted, "Watch me, Esslie, I can jump over this!" And he started running towards the pond. I jumped up, but Adrian shouted from the top of the ladder, "It's all right, Elsie, he knows not to go too near it." But I knew different. Jamie was showing off for me. It would make him reckless. So I ran after him.

Pause

I never meant to smack him, I swear I never meant to. It all happened so quickly. He was teetering on the edge, shouting "Watch me, Esslie, watch me!" I shouted to him not to move. But he started to jump, and I grabbed him, and God forgive me, I gave him a hard slap across the back of the legs. Oh, the silence. Everything froze ... everything was fixed. Kate's shocked face in the kitchen window. Adrian looking down from the ladder. And Jamie's big blue eyes, full of tears. He didn't cry. He just looked up at me as if he couldn't believe Esslie could hurt him like that. And then everything started moving again. Adrian slid down the ladder, came barging over and pushed me to one side, and picked Jamie up. That's when Jamie did start to cry. And Adrian said, "How dare you, how dare you hit my child ... " Then Kate was there and I expected her to scream and yell at me. But she just said, "I think you should go, Elsie." She walked to the gate with me and I tried to explain, but she just said how smacking might have been fine for my generation, but she could never condone any form of physical violence. Physical violence! I mean, if you had a choice between giving a child a smack and letting him drown, what would you do? I felt sick. I got a terrible migraine, I had to lie down for the rest of the day. Jamie hasn't been round since. I see him sometimes, playing in the garden, and he waves to me, bless him. Children forget very quickly. But he's never been near.

She tries to smile

It's a shame! Because I remembered the rest of that dragon song, I wanted to sing it to him.

She sings, sadly, the last verse of "Puff the Magic Dragon"

Something catches her eye. She leaps up and goes back to the window

They're coming out of the house now. Oh, look at him! First day at school. Bless his heart. All grown up, with his uniform and his tidy hair. Kate's taking a photo of him. Off they go. He's holding her hand … that won't last.

She turns away from the window

I was supposed to be there with them. I'd have been in the photograph. And Jamie might look back on it in ten years' time and he might remember funny old Esslie who taught him silly songs and made him cocoa. I was supposed to be there ... I've learned my lesson. It doesn't do, to get involved. I shan't do it again.

She sits down, and the doorbell rings. Joy and hope cross her face, she leaps up and practically runs off stage

Music begins: "Orange-Colored Sky" by Nat King Cole

After a moment, Elsie enters. She is holding the lunch box she bought for Jamie, which Kate has obviously left outside on the step. She sits with the lunch box, and weeps

The Lights fade

END

FURNITURE AND PROPERTY LIST

On stage: Chair
              Newspaper

Offstage: Tray. *On it*: small teapot, china cup and saucer, milk jug,
                   plate of biscuits, letter in airmail envelope (**Elsie**)
              Small card (**Elsie**)
              Tray. *On it*: tea, toast
              Bright tin of buttons, pile of comics, **Elsie**'s china cup,
                   mug with "World's Best Grandad" printed on it,
                   biscuit barrel, enormous bunch of keys
                   (**Elsie/Stage Management**)
              Bought sandwich, carrier bag containing brightly-coloured
                   lunch box, handbag containing tissue (**Elsie**)

LIGHTING PLOT

Practical fittings required: nil

To open: General interior lighting

Cue 1	**Elsie**: "Postman." *Fade Lights*	(Page 2)
Cue 2	**Elsie** enters *Bring up Lights*	(Page 2)
Cue 3	**Elsie**: "We move on." *Fade Lights to black-out*	(Page 5)
Cue 4	When ready *Bring up Lights*	(Page 5)
Cue 5	**Elsie** exits *Fade Lights*	(Page 7)
Cue 6	**Elsie** enters *Bring up Lights*	(Page 7)
Cue 7	**Elsie**: "Nice name." *Black-out*	(Page 8)
Cue 8	**Elsie** enters *Bring up Lights*	(Page 8)
Cue 9	**Elsie** calmly eats her toast *Fade Lights to black-out*	(Page 10)

EFFECTS PLOT

To open: *Puff the Magic Dragon* by Peter, Paul and Mary plays

Cue 1	**Elsie**: "All the more shortbread for me, then." *Noise of postman, off*	(Page 2)
Cue 2	The Lights fade to black-out *"Who's Afraid of the Big Bad Wolf" by Henry Hall plays*	(Page 5)
Cue 3	**Elsie**: "But without the "hope" bit." *Doorbell rings, off*	(Page 6)
Cue 4	Black-out *"Nellie the Elephant" by Mandy Miller plays*	(Page 8)
Cue 5	**Elsie**: "... no point in setting the table just for me." *Doorbell rings*	(Page 10)
Cue 6	**Elsie**: "I've proved it." *Doorbell rings again a few times*	(Page 10)
Cue 7	The Lights fade *"Little Boy Fishing" by Shirley Abicair plays*	(Page 10)
Cue 8	The Lights fade *"Bring Me Sunshine" by Morecambe and Wise plays*	(Page 13)
Cue 9	Black-out. **Elsie** exits *"Gilly Gilly Ossenfeffer Katzenellen Bogen by the Sea" by Max Bygraves plays*	(Page 15)
Cue 10	**Elsie** practically runs off stage *"Orange-Colored Sky" by Nat King Cole plays*	

www.ingramcontent.com/pod-product-compliance
Ingram Content Group UK Ltd.
Pitfield, Milton Keynes, MK11 3LW, UK
UKHW021820150726
7214IPUK00017B/223